Anger Management

How to Handle Your Angry Feelings for the Sake of Your Relationships and Your Own Personal Development

(Learn how to avoid falling into the rage trap, gain control of your emotions, and strengthen your relationships)

Vladimir Kohl

TABLE OF CONTENT

Introduction..1

Anger Is A Natural, Primary Emotion Just Like Sadness, Contentment, And Happiness. Anger Usually Presents Itself In A Hasty Manner, And Usually Leaves A Person Feeling Uncomfortable And Uneasy. One Can Tell What Is Anger? 4

The Outward Signs Of Angry Emotions And Their Repercussions On The Body..........................8

Take Immediate Action, Or Someone Will Be Hurt: Here Are Some Useful Techniques That May Help You Keep Your Emotions Under Control. 14

Instead Of Trying To Manage Your Anger, Try To Deal With It..18

A Closer Look Through A Magnifying Glass At The Emotion Of "Anger"..29

It's All About Fury Here. 35

Effectively Expressing Yourself To Others.......38

How Can I Prevent My Anger From Getting The Best Of Me?..43

Managing Anger In The Company Of Good Friends 56

How Does The Anger Tree Cultivate Its Fruits? 62

Seeking Treatment From A Doctor 68

Counseling For The Management Of Anger 74

Listen For The Warning 78

Put An End To Fury Before It Starts 89

It Is Ok To Have Both Positive And Negative Feelings. 93

What Exactly Is A Healthy Level Of Anger? 98

How To Make Sense Of Your Child's Temper Tantrums 106

The Person Who Throws A Tantrum 115

Feelings Should Be Discussed. 122

A Dissection Of The Angry Brain 130

The Roots Of Children's Angry Behavior 136

The Truth Behind Anger And Its Many Myths 142

Put An End To Your Anger Before It Ever Begins. 148

Introduction

This book will present you with everything you need to get started on your path towards a life that is not longercharacterised by anger, and it will do so in order to assist you on your trip. You will start by gaining a comprehensive understanding of rage and the ways in which this much-maligned emotion truly does receive a poor name. The next lesson will teach you everything about the fundamentals of anger management, as well as how you can immediately begin putting yourself in a position to have a more fruitful future.

After that, you will get an understanding of the primary types of rage, as well as the fundamental methods for responding to each kind. You will discover chapters in this book that are dedicated to both the physical and mental skills that you may use to assist yourself cope with anger in an effective manner. These chapters will provide you with even more helpful approaches. In the last section, you will discover some extra advice that will assist you in the long-term management of your anger.

Before you get started, it is essential to bear in mind that everyone feels anger in their own unique way. Because of this, the strategies that are going to be effective in addressing anger will also vary from person to person. All of this is to imply that if one or more of the strategies that are given on the subsequent pages do not work for you, it is essential to avoid becoming disheartened and to instead put your head down and continue trying other strategies until you discover one that sticks. As long as you don't give up, you'll soon have a whole new and healthier connection with anger before you ever realise it. The answer that's just suited for you is sure to be lurking around here someplace.

Anger Is A Natural, Primary Emotion Just Like Sadness, Contentment, And Happiness. Anger Usually Presents Itself In A Hasty Manner, And Usually Leaves A Person Feeling Uncomfortable And Uneasy. One Can Tell What Is Anger?

whether they are furious by the way they feel, the way they carry themselves, or the comments they provide verbally. Some individuals mistakenly internalise their sentiments of rage, which may leave them feeling irritated or upset without having a clear knowledge of why they are experiencing those things.

Even the feeling of rage itself does not provide a challenge. When it comes to dealing with intense emotions of anger, the most important thing to focus on is how you choose to respond to the emotion when it arises. There are often two levels of anger that present itself, and these are called mild anger and wrath respectively.

It's possible that mild anger is merely an irritant, but if it's not handled, it might easily escalate into wrath. Rage may be defined as an extreme kind of rage. It's possible that it might lead someone to act in a way that's detrimental to themselves or to others.

On several instances, one may experience a level of mild rage. It's possible that you're feeling hungry or fatigued; if so, getting a good night's sleep or eating something will immediately make your irritated sensations go away.

If you feel humiliated or criticised by a co-worker at work or a loved one, you may experience sentiments of moderate rage. These feelings may be brought on by either situation. It's possible that just letting out some steam can put you in a better mood.

Because rage often represents sentiments that a person has been experiencing for a considerable amount of time, its intensity may be fairly high. A person may have grown incredibly adept at concealing their emotions, until one day, out of nowhere, their rage bursts and they lose control of themselves.

Because it prompts the body to go into flight or fight mode almost instantly, anger may wreak havoc on a person's physical health. Hormones that are associated with stress are secreted, one's pulse quickens, and their blood pressure rises. If a person is constantly confronted with these powerful emotions, there is a good chance that they are putting their body through significant stress and suffering.

Regardless, anger is a feeling that has to be expressed at some point. If it isn't properly communicated, anger may easily transform into sadness. Depression occurs when a person holds on to the pain they are feeling, which may lead to a variety of psychological issues.

Anger is a warning indication that something is not right, so pay attention to it. It's possible that you've worked out what's wrong, but it's also possible that you have no idea what's giving you such a bad attitude.

I want to do all I can to assist you in determining the source of the powerful emotions you're experiencing so that you can put an end to them once and for all.

The Outward Signs Of Angry Emotions And Their Repercussions On The Body

Do you not believe you are facing any difficulties? What about the other persons in the room with you? Did you know that there is such a thing as an anger disorder, and that it is possible for anybody to be affected by it at any given time? It is a fact that a person who is constantly or excessively angry has a problem, and in order to assist them, it is necessary to address their anger issues. It is not a sign of weakness to own that you have such a problem; we are not in complete command of our emotions, particularly when they go into overdrive.

The most essential skill to have in this context is the capacity to recognise anger for what it is and to differentiate between normal, healthy, occasional anger and the kind of fury that is caused by a problem that may have a profound impact on one's whole life. Anger disorders come in a wide variety, and it is crucial for you and the people you contact with, such as friends, family, and coworkers, to be able to identify the specific kind of anger problem that you have.

Different kinds of rage disorders

Anger that you inflict on yourself is often brought on by feelings of guilt, and it is directed inward.

Anger that lasts for an extended period of time and is often associated with various forms of mental illness is referred to as chronic anger. This sort of anger may have a significant effect on a person's immune system.

Anger that is prone to explosive outbursts, which is perilous and hard to anticipate since it develops out of nowhere and is characterised by inappropriate and excessive levels of violence.

Anger that is caused by a someone having too much duty, too many demands, or too much emotional damage may be described as "overwhelmed."

rage that is fueled by feelings such as bitterness, jealously, or other negative emotions is referred to as judgmental rage.

It is difficult to identify passive rage since it does not behave in the same way that ordinary anger does.

You need to be aware that anger may be broken down into two broad categories in order to be able to appropriately diagnose an anger issue. These two categories are known as passive anger and aggressive anger, respectively. The two are not at all comparable, and each comes with its own distinctive collection of illustrative particulars. You need to be familiar with the primary distinctions between them, in addition to the normal symptoms of each, in order to accurately diagnose either yourself or another individual.

a rage that is aggressive

The form of rage that is loud and evident is called aggressive anger. It makes its presence known in an obvious way, both loudly and physically. Sometimes, depending on how intense the anger is, it may also become violent — either towards other people, against oneself, or even towards objects or animals. This can happen either towards other people or towards oneself. This is the sort of fury that can be seen by anybody, due to the fact that the indicators are obvious not only in behaviour and attitude, but also in the physical body.

Aggressive rage is simple to recognise because it is so blatant and clear; as a result, coming to terms with the fact that you have a problem is a rather straightforward process. We are all able to point our fingers at the person who is upset because they are the ones who have a red face with a bulging vein running across their forehead. Additionally, they are the ones who are throwing staplers across the office and yelling at interns.

Anger held in check

On the other hand, being aware of someone's passive rage is much more challenging due to the fact that it is more covert. Instead of striking out, you let your feelings to percolate inside of you. Because there is no outward sign of your anger, in point of fact, you may not even be aware that it exists inside you because there is no visible expression of it. There is no kicking and yelling, but there is overall meanness, sarcasm, and covertly taking pleasure in the pain of other people.

Because it is not at all visible, some would attempt to suggest that passive anger is, in fact, maybe more deadly than aggressive anger. This is due to the fact that passive anger is more difficult to see. Nobody outside of you is aware of the feelings that are developing inside you; sometimes, you aren't even aware of them yourself. This might not only lead to stressful situations with other people, but it can also lead to health concerns that may go unnoticed or unsolved for lengthy periods of time. This can have a negative impact on both your mental and physical health.

Take Immediate Action, Or Someone Will Be Hurt: Here Are Some Useful Techniques That May Help You Keep Your Emotions Under Control.

An intervention for anger management will be broken down into its component parts during the course of this chapter. This will provide you with actionable advice that can be applied on a daily basis to help you keep your anger under control and reduce the frequency with which you engage in violent behaviour.

Calmness and ease

This technique involves soothing both your body and your thoughts at the same time. Due to the fact that they are intertwined, the unease that is experienced by one will also have an effect on the other. In addition, the following are some easy measures that a person may do in order to achieve a state of relaxation:

Learn how to practise deep breathing. The most effective technique to breathe is to take air from the diaphragm, rather than relying on the lungs, much as singers do. When oxygen is introduced into your whole body, the physiological processes that are taking place inside of an individual's body have a tendency to gradually become more subdued and return to their initial condition. One may sign up for a class in either yoga or tai chi, which are both forms of exercise that use such method, in order to completely acquire such skill.

The person may find it easier to relax if they learn to cease their thoughts. This is the way of making a conscious effort to stop your mind from thinking of anything that can remind you of anything that is linked to your object of frustration, such as the person who caused it or the scenario where it occurred. This is the method of stopping your mind from thinking of anything that may remind you of anything that is related to your object of irritation.

Imagine yourself in a calm and relaxed setting in order to engage in the practise of visualisation. You might apply this after you have stopped thinking about the stressful circumstance, since the person will be better able to think about the tranquil situation after you have stopped your thoughts from thinking about the stressful one.

You should try to educate yourself on how to massage various sections of your body if at all feasible. In severe circumstances, individuals may feel as if they have strain all over their body as a result of the stress. Therefore, if your body is not going through such pressures, it might make it easier for your mind to rest.

It is essential to put these skills into practise in every aggravating circumstance that you may face in the future. The more you practise it, the more it will become ingrained in your routine, which will enable you to maintain your composure no matter how stressful the situation was before you began to practise relaxing.

Instead Of Trying To Manage Your Anger, Try To Deal With It.

One of the most potent, self-destructive, and damaging feelings that a human being is capable of experiencing is anger. It is possible for it to have a significant impact on one's life if it is not dealt with in the appropriate manner.

Anger may be caused by a variety of factors, including the stresses of one's job and family life as well as the inappropriate actions of others. When it is not addressed, rage may give rise to a powerful need to do something destructive.

One day, after returning home from work, a guy had a sudden outburst of rage directed at his wife, who was still at work. After seeing his wife exit the car driven by the guy who had brought her home, his rage turned into resentment, and he became verbally abusive towards the man. As soon as his wife entered the residence, he questioned her on the individual who had brought her there. Her response, which was met with complete and total bewilderment, was "of course, your uncle." It was not the first time that his uncle had brought her back to the house.

He got out his phone and dialled his uncle's number to ask him to verify what his wife had said to him. The man's uncle, who had no idea that the man would suspect that his wife was having an affair with another guy, confirmed that the account given by the wife was accurate. Unhappily, the man's rage did not begin to abate at any point.

While the husband was busy formulating a plan in his head for taking out his frustration on his wife, the woman walked upstairs to change. After she had finished changing and returned to the basement, she began serving the meal. The guy at the table was not eating since he was too occupied gazing at his wife the whole time they were there. When the man's wife saw that he was starring at her instead of eating, she confronted him with the question, "Why are you staring at me?"

The guy responded with a query along the lines of "Do you know that I can pour this hot soup on you?"

The lady was under the impression that he was kidding and responded by saying, "If you pour it, you will eat the food from my body."

The guy, who was now over himself with rage, grabbed the dish he had been eating from and threw it over his wife. He snatched a knife off the table, where it had been lying, and stabbed the lady, reasoning that she would respond in like. When this occurred, the family's youngest daughter, who was under the age of eighteen at the time, began screaming, which caused the neighbours to become concerned. As soon as they entered their flat, they saw the lady lying in a pool of her own blood. Others carried the guy to the police station as still others transported the lady to the hospital in an ambulance. Sadly, the lady passed away as she was being transported to the hospital.

The guy constantly sobbed while he was in the custody of the police and said that he had no idea what had gotten into him. He said that he loved his wife and that this was the first time he had ever touched her. Even if the guy was given a just punishment of five years in jail because of their little kid, he will undoubtedly spend the rest of his life living with the remorse of the moment of fury that he caused.

Many families have been ruined because of anger. According to a quote attributed to Eleanor Roosevelt, "The term 'Anger' is one word short of 'D-anger. That is correct. When hostility is allowed to fester, there is always the possibility of disastrous outcomes.

I heard of a dad who tossed his daughter off of a three-story building where they resided because he caught her having an affair with her lover in his marital bed. The man flung his daughter off the building because he spotted her having the affair in his bed. It's true that he had the right to be upset, but you'll probably agree with me when I say that his actions went well too far.

Because of their rage, some individuals have been unable to access the door that would have allowed them to go to the following level. Some people have taken their fury out on the people they love the most. Because of their rage, some people have broken the confidence of their close friends and family members.

The emotion of anger is a demon. It is a monster that we must learn to drive away and fight against with all that we have. It is one of the most lethal weapons in Satan's arsenal for destroying people's lives.

Because of a few minutes of out-of-control rage, many individuals who have bright futures ahead of them are now languishing in the police net. Anger that is allowed to fester has a high likelihood of becoming poisonous, which will ultimately cause the vessel it is contained in to burst. Because of this, the Word of God does not let your wrath to linger for one more day.

Day 10: Learn to Care and Forgive Those Who Have Hurt You

Learning how to really care for and forgive other people is one of the most important steps you can take towards gaining better control of your anger. However, this is also one of the most difficult steps. Anger may be caused by a number of circumstances, including harbouring resentment and a lack of empathy for others. On the other hand, trying to comprehend how other people feel by experiencing those feelings via the perspective of another person might assist. Consider the individuals in your life that bring you down or make your life more difficult. Is it possible that destroying them will make things better? Do you want others to forgive you and treat you properly if you've hurt their feelings in any way or made a mistake in front of them? If you give yourself permission to care about and forgive other people, it will be easier for you to keep your anger under control and may also help you see the wider picture.

Ask yourself what it is that you are actually becoming irritated and furious about if you find that your anger and annoyance levels are rising. Discovering the source of your annoyance will make it easier for you to express the sensation in a manner that is productive and to come up with a solution that will satisfy you. As soon as the fire of anger takes hold of you, it might be simple to hurl insults or other displays of irritation, either at yourself or at other people. This is true whether you are angry at yourself or at other people. It is very simple to point the finger at other people for the way you are or for the challenging areas of your life. Consider the here and now with an attitude of seeking answers to the problems you're facing, rather than laying blame for the past on other people.

If you find yourself becoming angry in a scenario involving other people, the next time this happens to you, remind yourself that it is more essential to work on improving and preserving the connection than it is to prove who is right. You will be able to respect the other person more as a result of this. Confrontations and confrontations are exhausting, so you should begin to consider if your anger is worth the energy it takes to maintain it. If you choose fights and arguments over every little thing, other people won't take your issues seriously because of how you handle them.

Without being able to forgive, it is hard to resolve problems, whether they be with other people or with oneself. Eliminating the pointless impulse to punish other people is necessary in order to make progress towards finding answers. You need to have the ability to let things go when they no longer serve a purpose for you to fully overcome your anger issue. If there is a topic on which you just cannot reach a consensus, you should commit to moving on. It is often advisable to walk away from a quarrel that is only becoming worse as it progresses.

Depending on how you choose to handle the situation, your pattern for reacting to arguments and differences at work and at home may either lead to rifts and anger or it can lead to trust and safety in the relationship. Building your abilities in conflict resolution will result in improved interpersonal connections as well as a reduced need for anger management on your part.

A Closer Look Through A Magnifying Glass At The Emotion Of "Anger"

You will come to the realisation and acceptance that uncontrolled outbursts of rage only do you damage if you think on the quotation that was just above and then proceed to investigate the consequences of being furious. Despite the fact that this is true, it is quite important to have an understanding of what anger is and how the normal or occasional expression of the emotion may grow into something that might be harmful.

Comprehension of Angry Feelings

Everyone, at some time or another in their lives, will feel the normal and fundamental feeling of anger. The most frequent reason for rage is extreme mental or emotional suffering. Anger is a stinging, unpleasant sensation that affects the majority of us when we believe that someone has mistreated, wounded, opposed, or harmed us, or when we are confronted with problems that prevent us from achieving our objectives. Anger is a normal human response to being mistreated, hurt, opposed, or injured.

Because of the variety of ways in which we experience things, no two people experience anger in exactly the same way. This includes how intense it is, how long it lasts, and what sets it off. Some individuals are readily provoked to anger (triggers), however the same stimuli that may provoke fury in someone who is "easy to anger" could not provoke anger in someone who is more level-headed or as easily or as fast.

Some professionals in the field of anger management claim that, on average, an adult experiences moderate or chronic anger at least once per day, and experiences frustration between three and four times per day. On the other hand, other professionals are of the opinion that the number of times a person becomes furious in a given day ranges anywhere from 10 to 15, regardless of how they feel or express their anger.

Even while anger is a normal human emotion, the consequences it has on your life and behaviour may be both positive and negative depending on how you react and respond to it. Anger, at its most fundamental level, is a signal that something in the world around you is not right and helpful to you. It is a signal that you need to be more aware of that element, and if you can, take action to rectify it. The way in which you respond to the signal has an effect on your life, as does the way in which your anger impacts your wellbeing and health.

Both constructive and destructive behaviours may be shown by anger.

Many of us make the conscious decision to respond to our anger, which means that we engage in rash behaviour anytime we are in an angry state. An illustration is provided here. When we are injured by another person, our natural response is to "act out," which might include yelling or even throwing items at other people.

"Reacting" to rage or, for that matter, any other emotion, almost never ends up being beneficial to us. What really counts is how we react, and whether or not we can make productive use of our feelings, even our anger. When you respond to an emotion, you are "choosing to reflect on the emotion/situation, to think things through, and to then take a more informed decision and action."

If, for example, you are upset with a friend who pointed out your weaknesses, you should not get into a heated argument with that person. Instead, you should investigate the criticism that your friend has given you and determine whether or not it is correct. If it is, then you should focus on improving the areas in which you are lacking and become a better version of yourself.

It is vital to understand, accept, and reflect on your anger in order to properly deal with it, and then to react in a manner that is appropriate after doing so. On the other hand, this is not something that can be guaranteed, and the primary reason for this is that the vast majority of us have been socialised to see rage as a maladaptive rather than a healthy feeling.

In addition, the way that we respond to anger frequently drives us to react impulsively rather than respond to anger; we instinctually hang on to it until it swells into something gigantic and monster, and this is because of how we react to rage. Both of these strategies for coping with rage are not only ineffective but also detrimental to your overall health and existence.

The effects of long-term, uncontrolled rage are examined in the next chapter.

It's All About Fury Here.

What steps do you take when you unexpectedly find yourself in a precarious circumstance? How about when you are already running late for an interview and all of a sudden come across an obstacle on the way, like a flat tyre? Or when the person sitting next to you on a flight that lasts for 14 hours doesn't stop chatting nonsense or slurping his drink the whole time? Or how about when you return home on a night that is unbearably chilly only to discover that the heater is not functioning properly?

What is your first response when faced with these circumstances? Do you make an effort to find an alternate route to reach your destination? Do you ask the flight attendants to move you to a different seat for the duration of the journey? Do you seek for an electrician that can provide a rapid remedy as soon as feasible and come into your home? Or do you raise your voice and make a spectacle in front of other people while ranting and raving, screaming, shouting, abusing others, and shouting?

It's inevitable that life will hand you some flat tyres and some irritating passengers along the route. However, it is up to you as an individual to meet and greet people and to approach these circumstances in the most reasonable way possible. You may do them in one of two different ways. Either keep your cool and think of a way to solve the problem, or lose your temper and make things more worse.

Anger may be found everywhere and in anybody, regardless of their background or station in life. At some time throughout the day, everyone of us will experience anger; it's simply that some individuals experience it more deeply and more often than others. There are circumstances in which one's wrath is warranted; but, in other situations, a person who consistently shows indicators of extreme anger may have issues with maintaining control of their furious attitude.

The ability to control one's wrath is thus essential in this context.

As you may have guessed from the phrase's name, anger management refers to the process of managing one's wrath or maintaining self-control. For some people, this may seem to be a simple chore, but if you find yourself in this position, it only indicates that you do not struggle with rage. Lessons on how to handle anger should be sought out by those individuals who struggle to keep a level head in the face of even the mildest of provocation.

Let's have a better understanding of anger first, including what causes it, how it manifests itself, and when it manifests itself, before we go on to discussing approaches and tactics for controlling anger and temper.

Effectively Expressing Yourself To Others

In spite of all the preparations you will make to prevent yourself from being upset, there will be occasions when you will need to air out your feelings not only to make yourself feel better, but also for the sake of everyone else. Those who suppress their emotions do so for a variety of reasons, the most common of which is the fear of offending another person; nevertheless, this is not a healthy behaviour pattern. In the end, it doesn't matter whether you're at work, school, or anywhere else; the ideas you have have an impact, no matter how unique they may seem to be.

Or maybe you are aware that someone is engaging in a behaviour that is morally reprehensible and that someone need to confront that person. But how can you safeguard against giving the impression that you are the villain in this scenario? Here are a few helpful hints:

Always keep your focus on the end objective. The sort of anger that serves a useful purpose is the healthiest kind. What gives you such a bad mood? It is important not to lose sight of the reason for your anger since doing so would only lead you to get consumed by your feelings. When you want to impose yourself, the first guideline you need to follow is this one: keep focused.

It is also helpful to let other people know what is making you so furious. This makes it easier for the people around you to comprehend the source of your anger in the first place.

Try not to let things bother you too much. If someone criticises you, you shouldn't automatically assume the worst of them. There is a good chance that there is a purpose behind what they are doing:

It is common for individuals to have opposing viewpoints to yours in certain settings, such as the workplace. It is not because they despise you as a person. They are only doing their duties and sharing their own views.

It's possible that's simply how some individuals are. You should make an effort to investigate whether or not the problematic family member has always acted in the same manner towards you and other individuals. There is a possibility that it is not just happening to you.

It's possible that they're having a horrible day today. They are susceptible to anger for no apparent cause, just as you are. In moments like this, all you can do is try to give them some leeway and give them some slack.

When things grow too hot during the conversation, there's also a potential that one of the parties may say things that aren't appropriate for the situation. Make an effort to be a better person and just disregard those things for now. If you feel compelled to answer, restrict yourself to making remarks that are directly pertinent to the topic at hand, and act as if the insults and personal assaults never occurred.

Fight with honour. On the other hand, you should avoid making impolite remarks unless it is absolutely necessary. Make sure that the only items you bring up in conversation are those that are directly related to the problem at hand, keeping in mind the source of the anger. Giving each other such low blows will not assist the conversation, which is already quite tense.

Remember: Manners matter! It is particularly crucial to exercise caution with the words you use when you are feeling furious. It is just as harmful and detrimental to fling insults at another party as it is to toss anything personal at them, even if you do it on impulse.

How Can I Prevent My Anger From Getting The Best Of Me?

The feeling of anger may be both healthy and natural. On the other hand, it could show up in ways that are disproportionate to the underlying reason. In some contexts, the feeling has the potential to impede decision-making, damage relationships, and bring about a variety of other complications. Learning how to control your anger may help you protect yourself from experiencing emotional distress.

The emotion of anger is a typical reaction for people who are faced with difficult or scary circumstances. It's also likely that it's a secondary response to something more significant, like fear, loneliness, or depression. Under some conditions, the sensation can seem as if it were plucked out of thin air.

A person's relationships, as well as their mental health and quality of life, may all be negatively impacted when they experience anger often and to an extreme degree. This can also have a detrimental impact on the quality of their life. Keeping resentment bottled up within and denying its existence may also have long-term repercussions.

In 2015, 7.8% of people living in the United States were said to have experienced "inappropriate, strong, or poorly managed" anger, as stated in the publication CNS Spectrums. This was more common in males in their latter years.

People may use strategies and techniques to help them deal with the things that set off their anger and respond in more healthy ways.

What exactly is the meaning of the word "rage"?

The fight-or-flight response, which is triggered in response to the perception of a threat or injury, requires the experience of rage as an essential and beneficial component.

When it grows out of proportion or out of control, though, it may become poisonous and undermine a person's quality of life. This can lead to severe problems both at work and in personal relationships.

Humans and other creatures, including other animals, often communicate their anger by making loud sounds, clamping their teeth, staring, or adopting postures that are supposed to warn imaginary aggressors. All of these different approaches are being taken with the intention of either avoiding or reversing potentially harmful behaviours.

Manage Your Anger for Its Many Benefits

Making experience of a way to control your grief is complicated and involves many different essential components. The method assists people in taking control of their life and overcoming the tremendous setbacks that are triggered by the manner in which one goes about marvelling.

Heightened Sensitivity

A significant portion of the time, confusion is what first sparks a person's sense of wonder and curiosity. The show of compassion will be aided by coordination, which will increase resistance and perception for opportunity gathering. The ramifications of amazement are often rendered obsolete by various methods of deliberate perception when there is the option to choose a situation that is compatible with each other's point of view.

Fresh Perspectives and Improved Determination

Perspectives are widened and new encounters are found when compassion is offered to a greater number of people. Instead of providing you with the reason for your difficulty and all of the factors that contribute to it, the method of management will provide you solutions. It is helpful in establishing caring and limiting changes in indignation to have an understanding of the one's experiences.

Reduced Anxiety

The loss of weight is one technique for managing amazement that might provide a little amount of breathing space in the process of creating experiences. As soon as your feelings are no longer able to control your brain, you will be in a position to take a deeper breath and let the tension leave your body. This is naturally by manner of method of and to a large extent owing to care, which minimises the risk of carrying out during a difficult and most likely angry situation.

Having an Awareness of Responsibility

An excellent component of the chiefs' therapy consists of making the most of an opportunity to demand responsibility with regard to your feelings and, as a result, the following path that they reason. The method recommends that people are able to take a clear look at a situation and accept responsibility even when it is necessary, without shifting the fault to another location.

Improvements in Health

In various scenarios, stress has a couple of detrimental effects on one's health and success. Better self-control generally depends on leading a more successful way of life, and this is automatically normally accomplished by way of method of particular function of the reduced cost of weight loss. In the meanwhile that you are gaining enjoyment in of a means to control your curiosity and lower strain, via manner of way of you then certainly are in similar manner reducing your number one signal, danger of headaches or perhaps coronary heart issues.

Take better care of those awful triggers.

The Fifth Street Counselling Centre provides excellent wonder the leaders for their clients. These are only a few of the many occasions that the board has successfully directed curiosity in a positive direction. Regardless of the method in which one enhances their very own specific manner of lifestyles and institutions, except you develop a miles conventional awareness of self and the fantastic way to cope with managing to aid provide super come to be your lifestyles, you won't be able to make your lives a super get to be. You'll be able to feel more in charge and ready to take on a variety of challenges if you manage your wonder using the same-day undertaking plans that are accessible. You will figure out a way to better influence your decisions, and maybe even do it in a more effective manner. in addition to this, you should be able to take advantage of improvements such as improved communication and significantly reduced amounts of work to do. You should experience a significant improvement in the quality of your life, including a marked reduction in the sensation of weight gain and a marked reduction in the physiological signs and symptoms associated with obesity. If you feel much better and are able to channel your rage in a constructive manner, you may even be able to earn recognition for your efforts in areas that are likely to be of the utmost importance to you, which will provide you with a larger overall sense of achievement and purpose. The verdict. The experience of shock transforms a person into a submissive named authority. The power to pick defenceless targets may be obtained by building up uncontrolled rage one baby step at a time. You may be able to practise having better judgement at the same time as you are being trained to control your contempt for something. Shock the board exercises are often anticipated to help channel the wrath in such a way that you do not lose command over yourself even though you are feeling moody.

The strain

In today's world, practically everyone lives a lifestyle that is fraught with stress. You may get the benefits of a longer stretch by applying pressure on the board. If you have a superior handle over oneself, you'll notice that it's a lot less complicated to maintain a vital suitable technique from specific situations if you wish to be troublesome.

Affective processes

Since the moment we were born, we have never been able to keep our feelings to ourselves. When we are younger, we often do not have a clear understanding of the reasons behind the things that are happening to us. If you've ever paid attention to newborns, you've probably noticed that even before they are able to communicate verbally, they show how they are feeling by their facial expressions and body language. This might include things like laughing, sobbing, snuggling, getting annoyed, and a lot of other feelings.

As we become older, we get better at identifying the various feelings that we are experiencing. We are aware of how we are feeling, but the most of the time, we have no idea why we are experiencing those emotions. In this chapter, we will discuss the several ways in which your emotions might be characterised, as well as how emotions include much more than just expressing your sentiments.

By letting us know what we're feeling in the here and now, emotions provide us with information about the many ways in which we might respond to a certain circumstance. Every day, we are subjected to a range of feelings, the most of which are transitory. However, some feelings remain with us, and their influence on our mood might last throughout the whole day.

It is very important to keep in mind that there is no such thing as a healthy or unhealthy mood. The only thing that should occupy our thoughts is the means by which we may control these feelings. Every person has their own special style of expressing their feelings. The capacity to comprehend one's feelings is essential to gaining mastery over one's emotional state and learning how to exercise self-control.

What exactly are feelings?

An emotion may be thought of as an electrochemical signal that travels through the body in a repetitive loop.

Our reactions to the things that we take in from the outside world are what we call emotions. You should remember what you discovered in the prior chapter, which is that our perceptions influence the way we think about the world. Every feeling that we have is important because it reveals something about who we are.

We need to embrace and acknowledge all of our feelings, which is something that the majority of us have trouble doing. When it comes to expressing our emotions, we have a tendency to be quite critical of ourselves. It is more helpful to figure out why you feel a specific way rather than to try to convince yourself that you shouldn't feel that way.

Affective States and Moods

Feelings are not the same as states of mind. Both of these terms are often used interchangeably, however they do not have the same meaning. Even if we only experience an emotion for a few seconds, it is possible for it to have a great deal of intensity. Emotions do not always remain with us for a lengthy amount of time. Because of this, they have such a significant influence. On the other side, a mood is something that may not be experienced as strongly as an emotion, but it lasts for a longer period of time.

It has been found that there are essentially six different sorts of emotions that each and every human being is capable of feeling. Multiple feelings are able to coexist inside a person at the same time.

These six sensations are joy, anger, fear, disgust, joy, and sadness in that order: happiness, fear, disgust, joy, and anger.

Managing Anger In The Company Of Good Friends

It's only normal that you grow frustrated with your buddies every once in a while. It's an important component of a balanced partnership. On the other hand, you need to be aware of how to communicate your rage in a way that is both suitable and will not jeopardise your relationship.

You may wish to proceed in the following manner:

Give your buddy the opportunity to say what's on his mind.

When your buddy is upset, don't dispute with him; instead, give him the chance to say what's on his mind. The outcome will be catastrophic if you refuse to swallow your pride and continue to push for a confrontation with him. You will undoubtedly feel shame over it in the future. If he continues to be abusive, you should inform him in a level-headed manner that you are unable to speak to him in his state and that you will speak to him after he has regained his composure.

Get out of there and give him plenty of space to collect himself so he can continue.

After then, you have the option of leaving in order to defuse the situation. Because of this, he will have some time to collect himself and restore his composure. Do not speak if you are the one who is now experiencing anger. When you are angry, you will undoubtedly make nasty statements. Words once said are never able to be taken back. They are capable of causing wounds that are notoriously difficult to heal. Therefore, you should go somewhere where you may find a constructive technique to reduce your rage.

Hold a discourse straight from the heart.

After either you or your buddy has had some time to collect themselves, the two of you will be in a better position to have a heart-to-heart conversation. You should either ask him why he's upset or explain to him why you're furious. You will then be able to address the problem by reaching a compromise with the other party. Keep in mind that everyone of you is required to provide some of your resources. It's important for friends to comprehend one another and have the capacity to empathise with one another. If you are a genuine friend, you would be aware of the reasons behind your buddy's emotions in this situation.

Rekindle the relationship between you.

You and the other person should make a pact to ensure that the situation does not return to its previous harmful state. Therefore, the next time there is a misunderstanding, it has to be resolved as soon as possible. By doing this, we can avoid it from spiralling out of control. If you are aware that you were the cause of the problem, you should apologise and make remedies.

Consolidate the ties that bind you.

You should probably make an effort to spend quality time with your pals in order to strengthen the links that exist between you all. Participate in a get-together like a picnic or an expedition that requires interaction. You might have a pyjama party for them at your house, or you could bring everyone together for supper. There are a myriad of activities that may be done to foster comradery among pals.

Do not allow a little disagreement ruin an otherwise wonderful relationship.

Will you be able to let go if your buddy chooses not to reconcile with you in certain situations? You may respond with something along the lines of, "Well, I did everything I possibly could, but he still refuses to talk." Did you actually think that? If you leave a piece of wood in the warm sunshine for an extended period of time, regardless of how wet it is, it will eventually become dry. In a similar vein, your close buddy who has distanced themselves from you. Keep on showing him your love and warmth, and he will realise that you are being genuine in your feelings for him. He would start to feel more comfortable around you again.

It's not easy to find someone you can trust. As soon as you make a friend, you should do all in your power to keep them by your side "through thick and thin, through good times and bad," since that is exactly what friends are for.

How Does The Anger Tree Cultivate Its Fruits?

If you understand how anger develops and how it progresses to the point where it seems as if you can no longer contain it, then you will have a better idea of how to regulate it and how to prevent yourself from acting in a destructive manner when you are furious.

Imagine that your feelings of rage are those of a massive oak tree with roots, branches, and fruits. The roots represent the underlying reasons of your anger, while the branches and fruits represent the ways in which you display that fury.

Now, let's look at each one individually:

1.) THE ROOTS: The Reason Behind Your Angry Attitude

Nobody ever loses their cool for no apparent reason. There is always an underlying reason, often known as the roots. Your emotion of anger is triggered whenever your children engage in actions that you consider to be inappropriate and then push on the source of the problem.

It is important to keep in mind that some of the behaviours that your children show today that grate on your nerves could likely be a natural part of their growth. This is something that you should keep in mind.

As parents, we often find ourselves acting irrationally and on autopilot, and we do not always take the time to pause and examine the reasons behind our anger.

If you have previously been primed, it won't take much for your children to set you off when they do anything.

2.) THE BRANCHES: The Channel Through Which You Express Your Fury

This branch is meant to represent all of the many ways in which you might show your rage. It might be that you shout at your children, scream at the top of your lungs, slam the door, punish your children, shame your children, call them names, lock them out of the house, or distance yourself from them. Any emotional reaction you exhibit in response to a provocation is a branch on the "anger" tree, which is a much larger tree.

At this juncture, it is essential for you to maintain control of your responses and avoid allowing the situation to spiral out of your hands.

Remember that your kids will always remember how you handled your anger and how you reacted when you were upset. This will always make a bad impression on them.

3.) THE RESULTS OR FRUITS: The Repercussions of Your Angry Behaviour

The consequences of how you express your anger, both on yourself and on people around you, are the fruits that your anger tree bears. The results are often unfavourable in most cases.

It's be that the sense of guilt you have about how you handled the incident is what's holding you back. You could be concerned about the effect that blowing off top would have on your child's self-image and esteem if you did it. If you do not make your opinion known, you run the risk of thinking that you are not disciplining your children enough and of being afraid that they may develop into spoiled brats.

And the display of your anger might have a negative affect on your children, causing them to shout back at you, get defensive, become violent towards their siblings or mates, become sad and withdraw from social situations, or grow up to be adults who lack empathy for other people.

It's possible that the results of the impact of your fury will be to establish a cycle of rage that never ends. They walk away to their room, shut you out, and recoil into their shell, while you feel bad about losing it and then might blame them for not behaving properly after all, and the cycle continues. You yell at your kid, he yells back at you, and you in return, now more angry than before, yell or scream or spank them in return. They walk away to their room, shut you out, and recoil into their shell.

But if you recognise it, learn to keep it under control, and find productive methods to cope with it, you may avoid the development of the results described above, the fruits.

Seeking Treatment From A Doctor

For some individuals, learning how to manage and control their anger on their own may come easily, while for others, it may be extremely difficult, and the best course of action for them would be to seek the assistance of a professional for their problem. A person who struggles with anger problems has the option of taking part in a variety of programmes on anger management; alternatively, they may decide to participate in individual counselling sessions. If you have attempted to learn to control your anger on your own, but you are still having problems as a result of it, this is an indication that your anger problem is significant, and it requires more than simply attempting to learn on your own. Because it is not something that can be learned to control on one's own, those who struggle with an ongoing kind of anger are strongly encouraged to seek professional medical assistance. In addition, as a person diagnosed with Intermittent Explosive Disorder (IED), the best course of action for you would be to seek medical assistance rather than attempting to control your anger on your own. It is in your best interest to get professional assistance as soon as you become aware that your anger is having a detrimental impact on your life. You have many options when it comes to getting medical assistance, including the following three:

Individual Counselling or Therapy

You may get therapy for your anger in a number of different ways, one of which is through participating in individual counselling. You may learn how to better regulate your anger by going to see a therapist for anger management treatment. Your therapist will assist you in working through the feelings and ideas that are contributing to your anger. You will be taught strategies and methods for controlling your anger during treatment, and you will have the opportunity to put these new skills into practise while under the supervision of your therapist. After eight to ten weeks of therapy, a person who has a high degree of anger may have it down to the mid-range, depending on how consistent he is with the treatment. If you want to get the most out of your counselling sessions, you can't skip any of them and you have to finish all your therapist gives you, including any tasks or assignments they offer you. You may make an appointment with a therapist at your local hospital or by going online and making a reservation.

Psychotherapy in Group

People who suffer from rage disorders in a similar manner are brought together for the purpose of group therapy, during which they are given the opportunity to talk about their emotions and listen to one another. Participating in group therapy may provide you with a number of advantages, one of which is the chance to grow as a person. These benefits include, among others, the opportunity to work on yourself. Individually, group therapy almost usually includes some kind of network support programme, and it helps you become aware that you are not the only one attempting to master the art of anger management. You will learn via group therapy that you are not the only one going through this challenge, and being aware of this will enable you to maintain your motivation. Patients participating in group therapy are often led through each session by one or two therapists who serve as the group's leaders. Everyone in the group has the opportunity to learn strategies that may help them learn how to better regulate and control their anger, and they can do this together. You may join an anger therapy group by inquiring with a therapist or a practitioner in the field as to whether or not there are any groups in the area that are open to new members.

Participating in a Group Support Meeting

In general, support groups are gatherings of individuals who have a common goal, such as learning how to better control their anger; these groups are organised and led by members of the local community. A support group may be beneficial to you in the sense that it can assist you in making connections and introducing you to other individuals who have previously gone through the same period that you are now going through. In addition to this, they may be a great deal of assistance to you by putting you in touch with others from whom you can get support and those who are also struggling with anger management in the same way that you are. You will have the opportunity to both receive and provide helpful bits of advise to other people in a support group, as well as to both give and receive assistance from other people, and to share both your challenges and your successes with one another.

Counseling For The Management Of Anger

You don't have to struggle through the challenges of anger management on your own if you don't want to. Counselling may help you get your thoughts organised, give you permission to be vulnerable, and provide you the space to work through your problems. You may get treatment for dealing with your anger in a variety of settings, including solo sessions, group counselling sessions, and numerous clinics. Which option makes you feel more at ease is entirely up to you to decide. A person may phone one of the established hotlines in order to locate a physician, therapist, or support group in their location or in the surrounding area. The wonderful thing about hotlines is that they are typically anonymous, much like the internet, where you can also discover a wealth of information about counselling groups, therapists, and physicians. Another advantage of hotlines is that they are free to use.

It is not a sign of weakness or weakness of character to admit that you need assistance; rather, it is a sign of the former and of the latter. It is not going to be an easy task, but nothing that is worth fighting for in the long run ever is. The struggle to overcome anger management difficulties and reclaim control of your life is one that is well worth engaging in since doing so will result in a dramatic improvement in the quality of your life.

Aware of When to Look for Assistance

You are the only one who has the ability to regain control of your anger, but you do not have to accomplish it by yourself. There are individuals and communities out there that are willing to assist, support, and instruct you on how to effectively deal with your anger. It is time to seek treatment if you feel as if you are out of control, have anxiety while thinking about the things that set off your anger, and engage in abusive behaviour. Talking to a therapist or a medical expert about your anger management difficulties is the best way to prevent your life, your relationships, and your health from being destroyed by the problem. In addition, there are anger management programmes available, in which individuals may get the necessary assistance and support in the form of group sessions.

Counselling Given by Professionals

A therapist who specialises in anger management will be able to guide you through the process of developing an anger management programme and will also be able to advise you on whether or not you should consult with a psychiatrist for further diagnosis. If your anger is caused by an underlying issue, whether it be a problem with your physical or mental health, you will need to seek the diagnosis and assistance of a medical practitioner in order to resolve the issue. If the psychiatrist believes that you might benefit from seeing other experts, they will propose that you do so to those doctors.

Listen For The Warning

What kind of action should you take if you are abruptly punched or slapped in the face by another person? Should you slap or hit him back, or should you wait for another opportunity to exact revenge?

Both of these are poor reactions to anger, and you could be thinking of doing one of them right now, or you might have already done one of them. Either way, you should avoid doing either of them.

So the question is, what should be done?

The level of venom that one feels does not always remain the same. It's possible that the anger you felt when you found out that your buddy had lied to you was less strong than the anger you felt when you lost your job.

This suggests that you may have responded in a different manner in any of these two scenarios. This brings you to the first stage in anger control, which is to evaluate the current circumstances.

When evaluating the circumstance, there is one aspect of it that you need to be conscious of, and that aspect is the degree to which you are feeling angry. Use a scale if you need to, but rate how you are feeling.

Put your current level of anger on a scale from one to ten, with ten being the greatest and one representing the lowest. If you judge the level of intensity of your anger to be three out of ten, then you are most likely annoyed; on the other hand, if you judge it to be ten out of ten, then you are most certainly angry!

Keeping an eye on the temperature of your emotions is analogous to checking the thermometer in your kitchen when you are preparing meals.

When you are certain that the meal has reached the temperature that you want it to be at, then it is safe to remove it from the heat.

A same principle applies to rage. As soon as you realise that the situation is about to reach a critical point, you should immediately begin taking steps to bring it under control.

The degree to which you feel angry determines the manner in which you will exhibit it. The farther up the scale you go, the more likely it is that you will behave in an aggressive manner.

Stopping yourself when you feel the rage building up in your chest is the most prudent thing to do when it happens. Put an end to whatever it is that you are now thinking and doing, and stand back for a moment.

Stop moving if you feel the want to fight back at the person who just punched you. Maintain a sidearm stance, turn around, and walk away from the situation. Turning your back on a situation does not make you a worse person, nor does it label you as a coward.

Walking away is an indication that you are gaining a solid handle on yourself, which makes you an even better person because it makes you an even better person.

In order to keep your anger under control, you need to bear in mind that the more furious thoughts you allow yourself to have and the more time you spend allowing yourself to feel angry, the higher your level of anger will rise.

Reevaluate how angry you are as you walk away from that individual and write down your thoughts. You are going to see that it is decreasing in a consistent manner.

USE RELAXATION, MINDFULNESS, AND MEDITATION TO QUIET YOUR ANGRY URGES AND FEELINGS OF RESENTMENT.

"Don't worry about it!" "Take a deep breath!" "Calm down!" The words are really easy to pronounce. Nevertheless, obtaining a genuine state of relaxation is a very challenging endeavour. In this chapter, we will assist you in comprehending some fundamental aspects of relaxation and educate you methods that are straightforward to put into practise. When you feel threatened, you have a natural and instinctive propensity to become furious and violent; nevertheless, relaxing may help you overcome this tendency.

However, in your reality, there are two extra aspects that must be taken into consideration:

1. The majority of the dangers you encounter in your day-to-day existence are not likely to endanger your life. As we've seen, the most typical source of anger in your human world is the feeling that you've been insulted, misled, misunderstood, criticised, taunted, neglected, or treated unjustly by friends or family members. We are aware that certain dangers, such as a robbery or another kind of attack, might result in bodily injury, but the majority of the things that probably make you upset are not quite as pressing as they may seem at first glance.

2. Because you are a human, you have access to resources for finding solutions to problems that animals do not have. You may look to the laws, the rules, and

the regulations. You have the option of taking your disagreements to a judge, a teacher, a friend, a parent, a mediator, an attorney, a small claims court, or any of a number of other venues. Because of these factors, it is often in your best interest to avoid fighting, freezing up, or retreating. Instead, you should focus on reaching a negotiated solution that is advantageous to you as well as to the other parties involved.

This is known as the Relaxation Response.

It will take some time to find a solution that is fair. You have to take a few deep breaths and try to relax. You need to take a step back and assess the situation. You have to overcome the instinct you were born with, which is to quickly fight, retreat, or freeze. You will need to choose an action to take. Regrettably, as we discovered in chapter 9, simple questions and statements such as "Why can't you just relax?" are not sufficient to induce relaxation. However, if you are able to correctly practise relaxation, it will slow down your emotions and provide you with the time to create a response that is more intelligent when faced with circumstances that trigger your anger.

Both the instinctive fight reaction and the automatic relaxation response are inherently a part of human nature. Certain chemicals in the brain are produced when this reaction is activated; as a result, you begin to breathe more slowly and have a reduced need for oxygen. Your heart rate and blood pressure both slow down, and your blood pressure reduces. You find that your thoughts regarding your issues are becoming less disturbing. The relaxation response may be triggered in a variety of ways, but regardless of how it is induced, those who experience it are able to think more clearly, behave in a manner that is more congruent with their beliefs and self-interest, respond to challenges with less impulse, and make more constructive decisions. One of the most essential things you can do to disrupt the anger cycle is to educate yourself on various relaxation methods so you can keep your cool in the face of provocation.

Keep in mind, though, that we are discussing the process of developing a learnt response that may be used to counteract the impulsive inclinations that you have to act. It takes practise, and it's likely that you won't reach the deepest level of relaxation until you've worked at it for a long. Practise is required. There are a lot of individuals who are able to learn how to relax on their own, but there are other those who find it simpler to work with an experienced expert who can speed up the process of inducing the relaxation response. No matter how you go about it, being more relaxed is a skill that should not be overlooked for its own merits. Your ability to cope with the numerous challenges that life throws at you may be improved, and the resulting calm in your body has long-term health advantages.

Put An End To Fury Before It Starts

Let's count to five... 10, one thousand, ten thousand, count them all. In point of fact, a great deal might go place before you ever begin counting. However, it is exactly where the risk is. You could end yourself saying something you wish you hadn't. You run the risk of causing harm that cannot be repaired. You could even bring about a permanent shift in the lives of both you and your kid.

Although we may not be able to stop ourselves from being angry, we are in control of how we respond to it. When we master the ability to exercise self-control over our responses, we are able to sidestep the most unpleasant aspects of rage. Because of this, it is very important to be aware of the factors that might precipitate the development of rage.

In this chapter, we will discuss how to recognise the signs that it is time to rein in your anger. We are going to have a really in-depth conversation on parenting triggers.

How might a better knowledge of the triggers that come with parenting help us better control our anger?

You have to understand that the topic at hand is not how to quell rage. Trying to quell fury is often a futile endeavour, comparable to stopping the flow of a river. The goal of identifying potential parenting triggers is to reduce the likelihood that we will let our anger to get the better of us.

Take into consideration the following:

If you anticipate that the river may rise, you should move to higher land. That is exactly what I want to do with this post. There is a possibility that there is not much that can be done to prevent the river from flooding. On the other hand, there is a great deal that can be done to forestall the terrible effects.

We are able to regain control of the situation after we have acquired the skills necessary to successfully recognise these triggers. In particular, we have the ability to diffuse a situation before it spirals out of control. Take, for example, the fact that your children are arguing with each other over a certain item. You've already had a challenging day at the workplace, fought through traffic, and been handed unfavourable information. You are already dangerously near to the brink of the cliff. The argument between your children is all it takes to send you over the brink.

Is there anything you can do to prevent yourself from becoming more angry?

A little amount.

Is there anything you can do to get a handle on how you're going to react?

Yes! There are several things you can do to keep yourself from veering off the path. The key to success here is being able to identify rage as soon as it rears its ugly head. From that vantage point, you will be able to regulate your responses to the best of your ability.

Please keep in mind that you are the one who controls everything at all times. There is no need to feel hopeless about the situation. Because of this, you have the ability to control how you respond to certain situations. However, first and foremost, it is essential to have an understanding of the parenting triggers that push your buttons.

It Is Ok To Have Both Positive And Negative Feelings.

What Does It Mean to Feel Negative Emotions?

A negative emotion is any feeling that contributes to you experiencing a negative mood. Common sorts of feelings that humans experience include rage, fear, sorrow, hopelessness, impatience, contempt, disappointment, guilt, and humiliation.

Robert Plutchik, a psychologist, named eight fundamental feelings in the 1980s. These feelings were joy, sorrow, trust, disgust, fear, wrath, anticipation, and surprise. These eight feelings may be broken down into four distinct categories of distress.

We have a tendency to dismiss the truth that unpleasant feelings are a normal and inescapable part of existence in our world, which promotes cheerfulness as a virtue. As a consequence of this, when we do experience these feelings, we wind up feeling more worse than before.

It is okay to feel sad or angry sometimes, and it is something that I want you to keep in mind. We live in a world where things are always changing, where various people come from different backgrounds and have varying values, and where we ourselves come from a variety of backgrounds. It wouldn't shock me if we had a disagreement at some point in the future; it wouldn't be because we don't get along or don't respect one another, but rather because we have divergent viewpoints, and we're probably not going to want to compromise on that.

People have died in wars for far less, and although we often wish that others could see things from our perspective, we are cognizant of the fact that this is not always the case.

It is OK to experience a wide range of emotions, including rage, pain, regret, grief, disappointment, and so on. Every one of these feelings has a purpose in helping us maintain a healthy lifestyle. Therefore, there is no need for you to feel guilty for experiencing such feelings. There are times when a circumstance occurs that stimulates these feelings, and there are other instances when the only way to cope with it is to respond.

One of my close friends is prone to crying, and if anything unfortunate occurs, you can count on her to start sobbing. I never did understand her tendency to weep or find it endearing, but one day I saw that it was her method of dealing with difficult circumstances and that it wasn't a terrible response. After that, I could appreciate it.

Sometimes we find ourselves in the position of being the focus of someone else's misdirected anger and emotions, which may leave us feeling depressed, disappointed, or just plain furious. No one is going to sue you for experiencing such feelings; what we're looking at here is how to regulate subsequent responses to these emotions, so that it doesn't wind up causing damage.

All of the feelings that we experience are there to help us develop and stay alive. Even if some feelings are unpleasant, every single one of our emotions serves a constructive purpose, which is the reason we experience them in the first place.

For instance, feelings of shame and remorse motivate us to make amends for our transgressions and do what is right. We can more effectively combat a perceived threat when we are angry. The ability to look forward and make plans is facilitated by anticipation. The ability to pinpoint the origin of a threat is one of the ways that fear might serve to keep us safe from harm. We are brought back to reality when we experience joy. The capacity to experience sorrow strengthens our bonds with the people we care about and our capacity to empathise with others. The feeling of disgust compels us to turn away from harmful behaviours.

All of these feelings are significant, since they are the driving force behind us making the essential adjustments that are required in our lives.

What Exactly Is A Healthy Level Of Anger?

This manual devotes a good deal of its space to discussing the negative aspects of rage. We take a look at the potentially explosive hatred and fury that comes from bottling it up within. We are in agreement that these are all forms of violence that are terrible. Because nobody likes to be around another person if they are always furious, the first one is going to produce a lot of issues in our relationship and in our life. Nobody wants to be around someone who is always angry. If we are not attentive, the second one may result in a significant number of negative effects on our health.

However, this brings up an important question: what level of rage is seen as healthy and appropriate? We are aware that anger is a natural feeling that everyone of us will experience at some point in our lives; but, how can we choose the most effective strategy to communicate and release our anger without endangering both ourselves and others? Where are they?

This is the rationale behind the contrast between assertiveness and aggression. The solutions to many of the difficulties that we are attempting to circumvent and the challenges that were discussed in this chapter may be found in aggressive behaviour. When you are furious and enraged about anything, you make the decision to lose your mind, start screaming and yelling, and act out violently so that you may get away with it. This is seldom anything that has such a pleasing appearance.

It is natural to feel upset, and people have a perfectly valid reason to want things to go their way all the time. At some point in their life, everyone person will identify with this sentiment. On the other hand, it is unacceptable for you to lose your composure and endanger not only yourself but also the others around you in the process. It's alright, because learning how to be more forceful is a far healthier and better approach to cope with your anger than doing anything else.

This is the optimal middle ground between being aggressive and being quiet and allowing things to just take their natural course. You will still be able to let your emotions out when you use this strategy, but you will do it in a manner that is respectful and caring towards the other person. They will tell you in a calm manner that they don't like the situation or what they did and said to them, and then the two of you will be able to speak about it and find out the best way to go in order to make things better. Instead of shouting and screaming and trying to intimidate the other person, they will tell you that they don't like the scenario.

As you can see, there are a great many various things you can do to learn how to control your anger; but, there are also a great many things that may go wrong when you are unable to control your anger in the appropriate manner. Learning how to properly care for your enthusiasm for expressing yourself rather than burying your anger deep down is the skill that everyone has to learn to master. This can be accomplished without causing damage to either yourself or others at the same time.

Here are six Zen approaches to helping you move over your anger:

If you put these ideas to use and then practise mindfulness, you just may discover the solution that is most effective for you.

Learn to meditate attentively in the present moment, not engaging in the rage that you are watching. Mindfulness has been shown to be an effective tool for helping patients better regulate their anger when used by psychotherapists.

Pay heed to the compassion that other people show you, but ignore the unkindness that others show you.

Put your adversaries first in your meditations while you do Metta, which means loving-kindness and compassion for all creatures. One kind of Buddhist meditation is called the Metta meditation. "Metta" translates to "positive energy" and "kindness towards others" in the ancient Indian language of Pali, which is closely connected to the Sanskrit language and is spoken in northern India.

When dealing with other people, use knowledge and patience. Analysing should be done in a contemplative manner. If you are aware of the source and impact of the situation, and you go about seeking answers with time and patience, your anger will gradually subside.

The "substitution" strategy involves exchanging something nice for something unfavourable. To put it another way, if the behaviour of another person gets you furious, you should make an effort to shift your attention to the good aspects of that person.

Be present and aware. This is the approach that is suggested to be used the majority of the time. The oft-repeated adage that "the past is gone, and the future is not here yet" idea, along with relaxing the mind into an observation of the present moment...the 'now', is the method to get started with this practise. If you are trying to calm your mind but furious ideas keep popping into your head, just notice them without responding to them. Even while I realise it seems simpler in theory than in practise, I nevertheless encourage you to give it a go.

This is only a sample of how anybody may employ the practises of Zen meditation to fight off the unpleasant feeling that is connected with anger. The difference in the result will be determined by one's level of acceptance of the situation as well as their willingness to make changes.

It is possible to learn how to control one's anger; all that is required is an acceptance of the situation as it is, the identification of potential triggers to be aware of and to avoid, and the conscious decision to remain patient while working towards a desired end.

Look within to discover the source of your own inner peace and harmony between your mind, body, and spirit. This is the key that unlocks the compassionate human being that was intended for each of us to be from the beginning.

How To Make Sense Of Your Child's Temper Tantrums

Parents spend the first year of their kid's life getting to know their child's temperament and developing a relationship with their child. However, by the time a baby reaches the age of one, they are more likely to have temper tantrums, which may catch even the most observant parent off guard. A baby who is content one minute might suddenly start having a full-blown temper tantrum the next. This can happen in the blink of an eye. A parent is expected to maintain their composure in spite of the shrieks coming from their child. Irritation is the primary motivating factor behind the vast majority of outbursts. It may take some time for toddlers to learn how to articulate themselves, and the disconnect between what they want and what they are attempting to convey is often the moment at which a tantrum will begin to develop.

As a parent, when your child is having a tantrum, the first thing you should do is examine if the tantrum is being triggered by anything else, such as exhaustion or hunger. Babies who are subjected to excessive stimulation may exhibit disruptive behaviour as a result of their distress. If you become frustrated with your child, it will only make their emotions of anguish worse, not better. They lack the ability to exercise self-control, and they have a significant number of wants that are not being addressed. Children often do not acquire the ability to fully control their moods until they are in their late teens or early twenties. On the contrary, this is really how our brains develop in real life.

Their anger is sometimes warranted given the circumstances. Imagine if you are unable to get your hands on the items that you like. Jars are notoriously difficult to open. Everything in the world stands in the way of your progression through it.

As a result, the toddlers get agitated. For instance, your infant or toddler's tantrums might be caused by a variety of factors. You ought to have a few different replies. Saying something to the effect of "That's okay. " when you turn down something that they wanted to play with is one illustration of this principle in action. You can have some fun with it at a later time." After then, you would redirect their focus to an activity that you consider to be positive, such as building blocks or another activity. When they don't comprehend what you are doing, if you stay relaxed, particularly if you maintain your tone patient and peaceful, they will begin to figure it out. This is especially true if you keep your tone quiet. Children are similar to dogs in many respects. If you can divert their attention away from the item they desire, they will forget about it.

There is a good chance that they are becoming disinterested in all of their brightly coloured toys and are instead showing a lot of interest in other things. This behaviour is indicative of their intelligence, as well as their curiosity and desire to learn! There are numerous items that may be given to a newborn without requiring a significant financial investment on your part. As an illustration: Take an empty yoghurt container and place it inside of a closed shoebox. Do not add any other items to the box. They are going to get a kick out of ripping open the box and throwing the toy about. They are going to be overjoyed.

You might also take a paper bag and place within it a few toys that are suitable for kids to play with, and then give the bag to them. When kids seem to be bored or want to play with something that is intended for adults, all you need to do is collect some intriguing items to present them. They'll have pleasure doing that regardless of the discoveries they make, which is a blessing since they won't be able to check out what's inside the box until they remove the top. A baby handbag is another delightful accessory to have. Find an old handbag that does not have long straps and fill it with things that are comparable to what is found in your mother's bags, with the apparent exception of little objects. Toy items such as keys, sunglasses, and a mobile phone that resembles a kid's toy are examples of items that are safe for the child to put in their mouth. Even though it won't be long until the youngster finds it out, the purse trick is still a lot of fun for a lot of infants.

The fact that infants are only just beginning to walk is another factor that may contribute to their anxiety. It hurts just as much to try to learn how to walk as it does to go to the gym for the first time or to run five miles for the first time. When children first learn to walk, they are eager to explore the world and go places they were before unable to go.

As a result, they might get very upset if they are restricted from entering certain rooms, such as the kitchen. It's not a good idea to have a young child crawling about underfoot in the kitchen. At times like these, people are confronted with the reality that they cannot have what they want. The child's feelings of annoyance and frustration are very reasonable responses to the situation. You may reply by calming them down while asserting in a collected manner that they are wrong. Say something like, "I know you want that, but Mommy says no" before offering another option.

Tell them that you understand how they feel, but allow them to have their time even if they are constantly hovering over you while you are attempting to prepare. It wouldn't take the kid very long to grasp that weeping won't get them what they want in this situation. However, they need to be aware that you are not neglecting them in any way. It would be beneficial if you repeated yourself to them rather often. "Don't worry about it. I get that you're angry, and that's totally OK, but despite how you feel, your mother is not going to alter her decision. It is against the rules for you to be in the kitchen at this time.

Babies are happiest when their emotions are validated and recognised. Even before they seem to be communicating in their original languages, it is helpful to acknowledge the sentiments that they are experiencing. Think about producing some "fun boxes" to give to them in return for the stuff that they are not allowed to have, and be considerate of their sentiments while yet establishing the right limits.

The Person Who Throws A Tantrum

There is a good chance that you have been the target of at least one temper tantrum, if not more than ten of them. Temper tantrums are a natural part of a toddler's development and often manifest themselves when the child is overtired, hungry, or upset. Tantrums are an indication that your toddler is growing healthily, despite the fact that they may be difficult (and even humiliating) for parents to see their children engage in. Tantrums are often the result of the individual's growing frustration at their inability to adequately explain how they are feeling via words. Take a few deep breaths. In most cases, kids are just going through a period of growth that they will soon outgrow. Nevertheless, this type has the potential to irritate you unless they develop more patience and become better at managing their feelings.

For example, when things didn't go his way, our son Hans would throw tantrums. This happened rather often. One day, as we were strolling by a toy store, he saw a toy he desired displayed in the window of the store. Because we were already running late for his medical appointment, we were unable to pull over and wait for him at that precise time. We got a massive tantrum display smack in the midst of a busy sidewalk, as you could guess given the circumstances.

We were under the impression that our kid was the only one who had this behaviour until we learned how common tantrums are among toddlers, particularly those who are two years old. As children of this age are only beginning to acquire their language skills, they often resort to tantrums as a means of expressing their emotions because they do not yet understand how to articulate their thoughts and feelings.

Therefore, when your kid is acting out in ways that may seem extreme to you, such as kicking, weeping, biting, shouting, punching, or throwing objects, know that they are going through a lot more difficult period than you give them credit for. At this point, it is essential to make a habit out of maintaining your composure (remember, it all begins with you). Shouting and losing your composure will not help the problem and will only make things worse. Again, count to 10 in your brain, and while you're doing that, attempt to figure out what's making them throw a fit. Is your kid worn out? Is he or she hungry or thirsty? In such case, attending to the requirements in question could be enough to put an end to the tantrum. If nothing else works, you may always attempt to distract your youngster with anything like a tree leaf, a plush animal, or a bug.

The frequency of your child's temper tantrums should decrease as they become older. On the other hand, you obviously can't put off dealing with it for a few more years, right? We were unable to as well. As a result, we did some research, and the following are some strategies that we found to be effective when dealing with the temper tantrums of our children:

Move your kid to a place where there is less noise if your young child is having a temper tantrum in a location where he or she might damage himself or others.

Let your youngster learn from the experience of throwing a fit. Recognise and validate the emotions of your child. You should let them know that you understand the struggle that they are going through and that it is appropriate for them to be furious.

As a kind of diversion, you may go outside or take a stroll. It will be most effective for you to take this step when the outburst has just begun.

Try creating a goofy expression or joke with yourself. It's possible that if you use humour while your kid is having a temper tantrum, it will help to calm down their furious sentiments.

Have a chat with them when the outburst has died down. You should try to help your toddler figure out what is making them so angry. Reiterate on several occasions that having such sentiments is not abnormal. Ask them what caused them to feel that way while speaking to them in a quiet voice and then listen carefully to their response.

To reiterate, your child's temper tantrums are their method of expressing themselves. Good anger management skills should be taught to children as young as toddlers in order to assist them in the development of a more effective means of articulating their displeasure. You may do this by following these guidelines:

Start by learning to reign in your irrational outbursts. Since your kid learns from watching you, set a positive example for them by controlling your anger in a calm and collected manner. Because of this, it is essential to have plenty of practise being patient when dealing with their temper tantrums.

If your kid accomplishes anything that makes you happy, you should be sure to acknowledge it and provide your child positive reinforcement. "I couldn't be happier that you picked out your outfit all by yourself!"

Make sure you are aware of the distinction between their sentiments and the acts they do. You should try to let your child see that there is a constructive method to express their frustration. After your kid has had a fit, it is important to talk to them and explain that while they may feel a particular way, there are other ways to communicate how they are feeling. You may say something along the lines of, "I understand you had a really difficult time today my love, the next time you have these same feelings you can try to say, I'm really angry because..."

You'll be able to handle those fits of rage like a pro if you just have some patience and are willing to try out a few different strategies.

Feelings Should Be Discussed.

Feelings may be fairly confusing, particularly for younger children like a six-year-old who doesn't understand why you won't let him watch another hour of his favourite TV programme or an eight-year-old who is sad when you are called into work and their playground time is cut short early because of it. Because sentiments are such a conceptually vague idea, it may be rather challenging to explain them to children throughout their formative years. It is difficult to adequately convey what it is like to be afraid, nervous, enthusiastic, or even sad in words. It is of the utmost importance that you begin teaching your children about their feelings as soon as it is humanly possible to do so since your children's sentiments have a tendency to influence every decision they make throughout their life. Children who have a healthy understanding of their feelings are less likely to act irrationally or even throw tantrums when they need to communicate how they feel about something. A youngster who is capable of expressing, "my feelings are hurt," is in a better position to resolve a disagreement via peaceful means as opposed to lashing out in an aggressive way. Your ability to educate your kid about his feelings will be an important factor in the development of his emotional intelligence. Children who are able to comprehend their feelings and find healthy ways to deal with them grow up to be more self-assured adults.

Sentimental Expressions

It's a good idea to teach your kid basic emotion terms like "mad," "sad," "scared," and "happy." As your kid gets older, you'll be able to teach him more complicated words to describe his feelings, such as apprehensive, worried, irritated, or even disappointed. Having a conversation with your children about the emotions that could be experienced by the characters in their favourite books or programmes on television is an easy way to teach them about their own feelings. Take a moment to pause, and then ask your youngster, "What do you think she feels right about now?" After that, you may talk about the various sentiments that the aforementioned character could have and the causes for those feelings. It is beneficial to your kid's development of empathy if you encourage your youngster to speak about the emotions of others. As a general rule, children have the tendency to believe that the world revolves around them; thus, it might serve as a wake-up call for them to realise that other people also have emotions. Your child will have greater consideration for his or her playmates if he or she is aware that if he pushes a buddy while they are playing, it may cause the friend to get upset or even furious.

2. Recognising and accepting your rage

Because it may believe that anger has no place in the workplace, your organisation may suppress angry expressions. But the truth is that frustration and rage are common responses to everyday situations at work.

There is a high probability that employees will disagree with one another. Disagreement and even fury may readily be sparked by divergent points of view, methods of doing work, or ways of comprehending something. However, being aware of the ways in which you display anger may assist you in developing appropriate coping mechanisms for it and in avoiding the possible adverse effects of anger.

For example, do you have a tendency to overreact, so allowing your feelings to dictate how you behave and maybe igniting the tempers of others around you? Alternately, do you have a tendency to conceal your anger and instead vent it in more covert ways, such as by declining to take part in the activity? In any case, your anger is doing more harm than good.

Learning how to control your anger will make it easier for you to avoid expressing your anger in ways that are destructive or unproductive. You may get started by making an effort to comprehend the source of your rage. A good place to start is by examining the frequency with which you experience anger as well as the degree to which it affects you.

What Is It?

By providing a response to this question, you may get started investigating your anger. How often do you find yourself being irritated when you are at work?

Alternatives: 1. Not in any way

2. On a weekly basis, once or twice

3. Once or twice each day at most

4. Between six and ten times per day

A response

Option 1: It is likely that you are a member of a minority group in your place of employment. The vast majority of individuals have reported experiencing anger on occasion. Keep in mind that even the most subtle manifestations of anger, such as annoyance, are still regarded to be anger.

Option 2: It's normal to get angry once or twice a week. You shouldn't beat yourself up about it. You are going to have arguments with people and feel irritated at certain points along the process. It is really crucial that you articulate it in a suitable manner.

Option 3: Depending on the nature of the job that you perform and how well you are able to control your anger, it may be suitable for you to experience anger once or twice every day. Just be sure that you aren't doing more damage than good with your actions.

Option 4: It is not healthy to experience anger six to ten times every day. At this frequency, you will unquestionably have an effect on productivity, and you will find it challenging to collaborate with other people. Depending on the magnitude of your anger, there is also a risk that it will have serious consequences for your health.

According to the findings of Dr. W. Doyle Gentry, an expert in the control of anger, it is acceptable and good to feel furious anywhere from none at all to as often as five times each week. If you feel angry more often than this, you should investigate the source of your anger, look for methods to lessen your exposure to things that set you off, and educate yourself on how to control your anger.

Your level of intensity while expressing anger in the workplace is an additional crucial aspect of your anger. On a scale from one to 10, an intensity of six or lower is considered to be within the normal and healthy range. This is according to Dr. Gentry. On the other hand, if your score is greater than six, this is cause for concern since it suggests that you may have an anger management issue. Where do you believe you fall on a scale measuring the degree of anger?

When you consider both the frequency of your outbursts and the strength of them, you will have a more comprehensive picture of your anger and the ways in which it may negatively affect your colleagues, as well as your productivity and your ability to get things done in the office. Being angry may have major consequences for both your physical and emotional health. Allowing your anger to build up without addressing it is not a viable strategy, either professionally or emotionally.

A Dissection Of The Angry Brain

Your brain is a complicated computer that weighs between two and three pounds and has the consistency of butter. It is composed of water making up 75% of the total, brain matter which is composed of fat making up 60% of the whole, and an explosion of 100 billion neurons. Your delicate information processor is protected by a shell that is tougher than concrete and steel of the same mass and can withstand compression of more than 500 pounds. This shell is your skull, and it is one of the most important parts of your body.

The cortex of the brain, sometimes known as the "seat of the mind," is where conscious thought really takes place, however it only takes up one to four millimetres of space on the surface of the brain. Due to the various furrows and ridges that occupy the surface of the brain, the top layer of the brain has a surface area that is equivalent to 2.5 square feet. This is the terrain upon which conscious thought emerges, and it is upon this landscape that we develop strategies for dealing with aggressive impulses and feelings of wrath.

Both the left and the right hemisphere make up the cortex of the brain. The right hemisphere of the brain, which deals with unpleasant emotions, develops as soon as we are born because it assists us with meeting our fundamental requirements for existence. The left hemisphere of the brain, which is responsible for pleasant feelings, becomes completely functional sometime around the second year of a person's existence. Both of the brain's hemispheres work together to form the whole of the mind, which is what makes us whole as individuals.

The pre-frontal cortex, which is located at the front of the brain and directly behind the forehead, is the part of the brain that is responsible for managing anger and other strong emotions. Below the cortex and farther into the interior of the brain are other regions that participate in the processing of anger. These include the hypothalamus, which has a direct role in activating aggressive behaviour in reaction to threats, and the thalamus, which organises sensory impressions and provides the information to the cortex. Both of these structures are located deep inside the brain.

An information highway connects all of the different regions of the brain; neurons, which are responsible for communicating with one another and relaying information, move along this highway. The neurons link with as many as 10,000 other neurons all at once, and they organise themselves into chains. The connecting of neurons is what leads to the formation of habits like anger, which may then progress to fury. When anger becomes a habit, the neurons in a network that specialise in that region begin to gather in greater numbers and grow more powerful over the course of time. Inattention is the sole strategy that can be used to disrupt these neuronal rhythms. We can effectively starve them out if we reject their powerful urges to provoke us into aggressive behaviour; however, this requires effort on our part since the impulses they send us have a great deal of power over us.

The limbic system is located between the cortex and the brain stem, and it is responsible for the regulation of one's own emotions. Memory, learning, and the ability to control one's emotions are all made possible by it. It is also referred to as our "executive function," and it gives us the capacity to analyse all of the available actions, choose one of them, and then act in accordance with our selection. It is THE centre for directing and controlling our rage.

All of these different parts of the brain work together to either create order or encourage anarchy. The human brain is nothing more than a processor that is housed on a separate server. Because the server is dedicated only to serving our needs, we have complete discretion over the setting in which it is housed and complete authority over its administration. The majority of the time, we give its fundamental impulses the power to trigger and control us; yet, we have the ability to train it for our optimum advantage, and it would be a tragedy if we never even attempted to utilise our brains to attain their best potential.

The Roots Of Children's Angry Behavior

Anger has a variety of root causes that are unique to each kid and may arise from a variety of situations. As was said before, the eruption of fury might be the result of your kid suffering unjustified hurts and disappointment at the hands of others, including classmates or siblings.

Another possible explanation is that the individual in question has a fragile personality or character that has not been strengthened by you, the parent. Your kid may be selfish, for instance, which is an example of a bad character that they might have.

Your kid may develop pride, impatience, and a lack of respect for his parents and siblings as well as any other authority figure if he or she is self-centered. Your kid could have a strong urge to exert control over others as a result of the qualities described above, and as a consequence, he might be uncooperative and fast to get angry.

To facilitate a better comprehension of the factors that contribute to rage, we may break them down into two categories:

Aspects of your child's surroundings, such as emotional abuse, physical aggression, or neglect, as well as other environmental stresses

The youngster has a low degree of frustration tolerance, poor anger management abilities, and poor problem solving skills. These are things about the child.

If your kid has problems controlling their anger, then it is likely that they have been confronted with more fury than they are able to manage in the past. It is also possible that they have been subjected to an excessive amount of anger, which has prevented them from developing appropriate abilities for anger control. Let us take a closer look at the many factors that contribute to rage.

The pressures of the environment

Some of the difficulties that may be brought on for children as a result of their surroundings include the kid suffering the loss of a parent at a young age, being involved in a vehicle accident, or having trouble meeting their requirements as a result of their parents' negligence. Your kid may develop unhealthy coping strategies as a result of this, which might be a source of overwhelming stress and the reason why your child develops poor coping mechanisms to cope with additional stressful circumstances.

simulated actions

The behaviour that a youngster develops as a result of his day-to-day interactions with the individuals who are a part of his surroundings is known as modelledbehaviour. It is only fair to assume that your kid will acquire the same features if he or she is raised in the same household as other siblings who struggle to control their anger. It is essential that we provide a positive example for our kids to follow. The youngster will just copy whatever behaves appropriately in his eyes at that particular time.

There is a possibility that your child's anger issues stem from disagreements with their siblings. Conflicts between siblings are a common and significant source of tension in many homes. Jealousy, selfishness, an unhealthy level of competitiveness, insecurity, a negative body image, a drive towards control, loneliness, an inability to forgive, and consumerism are all possible causes of rage. These are only a few more instances among many more.

Abuse on all fronts: physically, sexually, and emotionally

If your kid has been subjected to physical or sexual abuse, then that youngster will likely acquire aggressive techniques of resolving any difficulties that they come across throughout their life. During the time that they are being abused, kids often have feelings of helplessness, but as they reach their teenage years, these behaviours become more obvious.

Behaviour that is aggressive and out of control emerges as a result of the frustrations that the individual may have seemed to have repressed for years. When you do not allow your children to freely express their rage, you are engaging in emotionally abusive behaviour towards them. It leads to the development of a kid who has weak abilities in the control of anger since, in the first place, the youngster may not even grasp what anger is.

The Truth Behind Anger And Its Many Myths

We have all had times when we have lost control of our anger, whether it was a thought outburst or an audible expression of impatience. After several unsuccessful attempts to complete a task, we have all experienced the helpless frustration that comes along with it. We have all had the experience of being very aggravated by the actions of another person, whether it be a loved one or even a co-worker at our place of employment. Yes, everyone of us has experienced our fair share of rage, and although the occasional release of that anger may be seen as beneficial, it is not something that any of us would want to do on a regular basis.

The issue arises, however, when any and all of these sensations become more often than "occasional." If you have noticed that you become frustrated or upset about the little things on a regular basis, or if you have been improperly lashing out at every irritated event, there is a good probability that you need to look into the need of anger management. If this describes your experience, read on. The mere suggestion that you may need help managing your anger may seem overwhelming to you. In a sense, it is a sudden realisation of how not only your mental and emotional health, but also your social life, is being harmed bit by little. This may be a scary realisation. This is the most terrifying part. You should take solace in the fact that you are not the only one. The thoughts and emotions that you consider to be practically difficult to triumph over are shared by thousands of other people who are doing so with great success.

Your ability to regulate, manage, and restrict your anger to a level that is psychologically healthy may be achieved with nothing more than the ideal combination of conviction and drive.

What Is It to Be Angry?

It is necessary to have an understanding of the nature of wrath itself before undertaking any efforts to fight its effects and repercussions. This is important not only because having this knowledge will assist you in recognising triggers due to the fact that you will be aware of the indications, symptoms, and severity level of the condition, but also because the therapy that you choose will be directly dependent on this information. In addition, it is of the utmost importance to acquire knowledge about the appropriateness of anger and to be able to recognise the thin line that separates a reasonable level of wrath from a level that has to be halted before it worsens.

Anger, an emotion that may range from moderate annoyance to intense frustration, can be perceived as a problem when it becomes a danger to ourselves, to people around us, to our property, or even to valued, intangible ideals such as a person's self-image, mental tranquilly, and social connections. This is when anger can be seen as a problem. Anger can vary from mild irritation to extreme exasperation.

In psychological parlance, rage may be broken down into three primary components, which are as follows:

The "fight or flight" response that rage elicits is a direct result of the bodily symptoms that accompany it. It is possible to classify it as one of the feelings that is associated with the most readily discernible bodily manifestations. When someone is angry, they have a rapid surge of adrenaline, which causes them to have greater blood pressure and a faster heart rate. This, in turn, causes them to have more energy and a desire to release it as quickly as possible.

The second component of an emotion is its associated cognitive process, which occurs both before and during the experience of the feeling. This includes any and all thoughts that serve as a catalyst for anger and that continue to make an individual feel aggrieved and irritated.

Behavioural - The last component is the consequence of this mental process, which is essentially the manner that we display our emotions. It is the result of the previous three components. Any behaviours that are shown as a consequence of these sentiments, whether they are as mild as just being silent or as violent as destroying property, there has to be a strategy to successfully regulate these responses, if not totally remove them. These reactions may range from being as calm as simply being quiet to being as aggressive as damaging property.

Put An End To Your Anger Before It Ever Begins.

The many expressions of rage were covered in the chapter before this one, along with strategies for determining which of them is most representative of your normal reaction. Now that you are armed with this knowledge, let's begin a step-by-step conversation about how you can put an end to your anger before it spirals out of control.

Because this is a learnt behaviour, you will need to relearn, or fully retrain, your brain to react in a different way in order to change it. You will need to disentangle your present response in order to do this. If you want to change the laces on your trainers, you must begin at the top of the laces and work your way down to the bottom. You cannot start from the bottom of the laces and work your way up.

Is it possible that something you learned when you were younger is the source of your rage? The following is a list of 'lessons' that are given to many youngsters and may have contributed to the anger problems that you are now experiencing as an adult:

If you respond with anger, you will get attention. If you respond with anger, you will get attention. Negative attention is better than no attention. The way other people feel is more important than the way you feel. If it might make someone else unhappy, you should not do it. Follow the rules, no matter how silly the rules are. Do not argue. Boys should not cry. Feelings are less important than logic. Keep your feelings to yourself. If you respond with anger, you will get attention. Negative attention is better than no

Children are often taught that their views do not matter and that they should "do as they are told" all of the time, which may be detrimental to their development. This does not foster communication or the healthy expression of emotions, and for many individuals, these attitudes grow into anger problems, which may leave them having trouble talking with others later in life. This is because these attitudes discourage communication and the healthy expression of emotions.

If you have children living in your house, you may want to examine the manner in which you interact with them and the words that you use while speaking to them. Your children should undoubtedly accept your directions, but it is vital to offer them the chance to comprehend why you want them to do things 'your way.' In other words, it is necessary to give your children the opportunity to understand why you want them to do something. It is essential to provide kids with a protected environment in which they may freely express themselves in any way they want.

Keep in mind that feelings are quite individual. They are flawless in every way. They are often mishandled and poorly understood, despite the fact that they are never in the wrong. Everyone, regardless of age, has to be made aware of the fact that their feelings are real, significant, and deserving of being understood.

Change the way you think about things, which brings us to Tip No. 8

The way that you think about the matter at hand is often the root cause of your outbursts of rage. And the habit of doing so may be extremely hard to overcome. The good news is that it is possible to alter the way that you think about the things that happen on around you, provided that you put in the effort to do so and are devoted to the tasks that need to be completed.

The first question you need to ask yourself is whether or not you believe that everything and everyone is an adversary or an impediment. If you do believe this, the next step is to examine why you hold this belief. It's possible that this is how you see the world, but it's quite improbable that everyone and everything is trying to harm you. On the other hand, if you look at things from this perspective, it will be quite simple for you to feel furious all the time.

There are a few things that you can do to increase the likelihood that you will be successful in altering the perspective that you have of the world, including the following:

When you first open your eyes in the morning, give yourself some time to reassure yourself that the day ahead will be enjoyable. You will speak to everyone, and you will approach every circumstance as if it were the first time you had encountered it. It is in your best interest to approach this without any preconceived notions or assumptions. If you start from scratch with everything, you will find that you have a far more positive attitude on life.

It is time to put an end to those unproductive ideas. If you catch yourself having a negative thinking, force yourself to interrupt it by shouting "Stop it!" to yourself. This assists in making the choice more aware, and it also increases the likelihood that you will stick with it.

Be sure that you are not concentrating all of your attention on how the circumstance is affecting you specifically. Instead of acting like way, you should consider how the other individuals involved will react to the anger you show. Consider the challenges they are encountering and the actions they are taking to overcome them. It is far less likely that you would place all of the responsibility on yourself or behave as if everything is a direct attack on you if you are able to direct your attention to the other persons involved in the scenario.

Your point of view will have a significant impact on the manner in which you respond to the events that occur in your environment. Those who have a lot of problems with anger tend to believe that the world is constantly trying to get them because they think the world is out to get them. Others who are able to maintain their composure are aware that this is not the case. If you educate yourself on how to become a member of the latter group, you will find that it is much simpler to maintain control over your wrath.

Anger is a typical feeling that everyone experiences, as was indicated in the beginning of this paragraph. When under control, it has the potential to be both beneficial and inspiring. Even if anger is a negative feeling, it is important to keep in mind the role it plays in our lives. It alerts you to the fact that there is an issue that has to be fixed as soon as possible. On the other hand, excessive and uncontrolled rage is a poison that may do damage in every aspect of one's life.

During the many years that I suffered with chronic anger, I would often justify my behaviour and dismiss the bad effects of my outbursts. During those years, I disregarded the negative consequences of my outbursts. I was aware, on some level, that my ongoing feelings of resentment were causing me undue stress and stealing away some of my joy. I also came to the conclusion that my short temper was negatively impacting my relationships with other people.

It has been said that anger is a wind that puts out the light of the intellect.

- Robert G. Ingersoll

Since then, I've gained the knowledge that it is normal for those who battle with anger to rationalise and explain the behaviour that they exhibit. Because of this, the first thing you need to do to get control of your explosive anger is to acknowledge all of the ways in which it has adversely impacted your life and caused your relationships to suffer.

Think about all of the individuals in your life that you have lost not because of the person that you really are on the inside, but rather because of the person that you sometimes project to the world. Think about all of the people that you have lost. Your outbursts of anger are not who you really are; rather, they are negative habits that you have developed through time. You will be relieved to know that you are able to alter these behaviours if you follow the nine steps suggested in this book.

Your ongoing battle with anger has undoubtedly caused you to alienate some of the individuals who were once dear to you at various points along the route. In addition to this, you have made things difficult for the individuals who have decided to remain here. Your lack of self-control in regard to rage has consequences for more than just you. Your tendency to become angry will almost certainly rub off on your children, and it may even be passed down to your grandkids. If you have children. You do not want to leave this type of legacy to the people you care about.

Not only is it harmful to the relationships you have, but it may also be harmful to your health. There's a good reason why so many types of media depict angry outbursts as the cause of heart attacks and other illnesses: such times are very dangerous. Your body goes through a lot of stress when your anger is out of control, and this may cause long-term harm to your health. Researchers from the Harvard School of Public Health found that having a history of chronic anger increases one's chance of having a stroke or a heart attack by a factor of three.

Anger that is out of control has been shown to lower a person's immune system, leaving them more vulnerable to illness and infection. Aside from these more spectacular occurrences, the everyday stress of chronic anger and the frustration of attempting to reverse the harm created by your furious outbursts may physically limit the amount of time you have left in this world.

www.ingramcontent.com/pod-product-compliance
Lightning Source LLC
Chambersburg PA
CBHW050234120526
44590CB00016B/2085